GW00691726

Tales from the Wedding Altar

True Stories from Las Vegas–Wedding Capital of the World

Rev. James E. (Jimmy Mac) McNamara

Christopher Matthews Publishing

www.christophermatthewspub.com
Bozeman, Montana

Tales from the Wedding Altar

Copyright © 2014 by Christopher Matthews Publishing

All rights reserved. Except as permitted under the U.S. Copyright Act of 1976, no part of this publication may be reproduced, distributed or transmitted in any form or by any means, or stored in a database or retrieval system without the prior written permission of the author.

Editor: Jeremy Soldevilla
Cover design: Armen Kojoyian
Typeface: Garamond

ISBN 978-1-938985-23-2

Published by
CHRISTOPHER MATTHEWS PUBLISHING
http://christophermatthewspub.com
Bozeman, Montana

Printed in the United States of America

This book is dedicated to my wife Lori
who knew we were in love —
long before I did.
And to all our children who manage to keep me
on my toes, keep me grounded
and let me know that I am loved by them all.
I thank God for each and every one of you!

Acknowledgments

Before I thank anyone I want to thank my Lord and Savior Jesus Christ by Whom ALL things are possible. I am proof that miracles still happen today.

* I want to thank my loving wife Lori whose faith, love and dedication (along with a LOT of patience) helped bring out the man in me that I needed to be as a husband, father and leader in our ministry.

* I want to thank my parents who decided to follow their Catholic beliefs and not abort.

* I want to thank Doug Loman, Associate Pastor at Valley Bible Fellowship in Las Vegas for giving me "the nudge" to preach my first sermon which led to my newly found career as well as fulfilling a calling I'd avoided for years.

* I'd like to thank my son Joshua whose love has remained undiminished and who has the drive of many.

* I'd also like to thank the many friends and extended family who have supported me, forgiven me and walked with me through this incredible journey in the Kingdom of God. If I get there before you do, I'll be waiting for ya'll.

* To all the wonderful and loving couples who have given me the honor to join you together – thank you!

Table of Contents

Introduction.. 1

Forgot the License? 5

Look Out for the Bees 9

Ball and Chain 13

Bagpipes 16

Bird Poop.. 18

Daddy's Rose 21

Doggie Shakes.. 25

The Archbishop of Canterbury 29

All Gas on Deck 32

Grand Canyon... 34

Granny's Gone Wild!... 36

Things Overheard by Family and Friends 39

We're Gonna Have Kids!...................................... 41

Motorcycle Mama 43

Lollipop Rings 45

Riding into the Sunset..48

How Did You Meet?..50

Cold Renewal 53

Jackhammer Tears 55

Lost Ring and Flames 57

Cell Phone Won't Float 61

Pink Socks..63

To The Dry Cleaners Now! 67

Gymnastics by Mistake 69

From Russia With Love...72

It's All About the Hair 74

From the Mouths of Babes 77

The Groom's Mom 80

Gung-Ho Bride 83

Things Overheard by the Bride and Groom...................86

"Let's Play a Joke on Him".......................................88

Belly Bump 91

"Yer Gonna Snip What?" 93

Just Another Day in Paradise....................................98

A Changed Woman 102

It Ain't Always Easy 105

The Haircut.. 110

Quotes from the Dads 114

The Rings? 116

Gone Fishin' 119

Free Ride in the Rain.. 121

The Brawlers... 125

Epilogue 129

From the Couples 132

About the Author 136

Introduction

I don't know really where to begin— I was born in New York although from my accent you wouldn't know it. Our family moved from Memphis, Tennessee, to Louisville, Kentucky, and back to Memphis where the "Big Divide" occurred. I got married and moved to Knoxville and then to Houston, Texas. Family landed in Nebraska, California and Georgia. After a couple of failed marriages, I moved to Las Vegas, Nevada, by invitation of a dear friend who passed away a couple of years ago. (Thank you Harvey—I've never forgotten you). I gained employment in "Sin City" quite easily as I had been in the plumbing and mechanical field most all my life. I was always driven by success. Having money and driving a nice vehicle and having a nice home was my definition of success.. I have always been a man of dreams and goals and never seemed to have the "right person" beside me to help accomplish these things. Little did I know that the "right person" would be a relationship with Jesus Christ. Having been raised a Catholic all my life, this wasn't something I needed ~ after all . . . I wasn't going to become a priest or a monk! However—having become a Christian and asking Jesus into my life in my mid-twenties, it was just a matter of asking Him to lead me instead of my own stubbornness. When this occurred, He led me to much greater things. My goals and dreams remain the same—but the rewards are much greater than fancy cars and mansions. He introduced a woman into my life that brings life and love and happiness.

He brought a new career that is so fulfilling—so meaningful and so great that even I don't have the words to describe it. And for those of you who know me— THAT is an understatement.

I've been performing weddings since the economic crash began in 2009 here in Las Vegas. A friend of my wife and mine is a Wedding Minister, and I had shared with him that my position as a Senior Project Manager would soon be over. Phil Larimore has been performing weddings in this town for going on two decades. He performed Lori's and my wedding ceremony and as a native Texan, we both spoke the same language. By this time, I had already been "called to preach" (don't laugh—it really DOES happen like that!) and was pastoring an outreach ministry from our church at an Assisted Living Center. I applied for my Certificate of Authority to Solemnize Wedding Marriages and performed my first ceremony within a week. I was hooked!

Having had a country band and performing on the Las Vegas Strip for almost 3 years (that would be the Brazos River Band for all you old followers) it was like being back on stage. I've always had the ability to have a quick comeback or to be able to use my wit at the drop of a hat. Some say it's a gift—others say it's a curse. Either way—it has helped me take claim to the title "#2 Wedding Officiant in the City of Las Vegas" —one that was bestowed on me by one of the wedding services online that serves this city.

Living and serving those in the Wedding Capital of the World is not only fun, but it gives me the opportunity to share some of what I learned at the expense of myself and others in my walk of life.

I've been doing my best to change the name from "Sin City" to "Saint City." In this book, you will stand beside me and get to hear what I hear as I stand at the altar as the Wedding Officiant.

In these pages, you will hear private comments between the bride and groom; from members of the wedding party before and during the ceremony.

Some of these were spoken loudly and some murmured and often whispered. Most of them are romantic, funny and oftentimes outrageous! You will notice that I do not mention anyone's names. The same as when I perform a Celebrity Wedding —all this information is private. I pride myself in allowing our couples to enjoy their special moments in a discreet way. If I have performed your wedding ceremony in the past, all I can say is thank you from the bottom of my heart for allowing me the privilege of doing so. I always consider it an honor to be the one chosen to share those moments with you.

If you feel any of these stories relate to you, then in the words of Prince Charming to Cinderella; "If the glass slipper fits . . . wear it!"

Forgot the License?

Can you say AWKWARD?! Oftentimes due to the emotional state of excitement and bliss, a wedding couple can forget a few things. One time there were the rings that were on the dresser back in Arizona. Another time the groom had to stop at the tux shop on the way to the wedding because he had actually "forgotten to get a tux" . . . and more times than you can imagine, they actually forget to bring the marriage license.

I've even had a couple that invited over 100 people to the ceremony, fly into town and get completely caught up in the whole "Vegas Experience", and fail to even buy the license! I performed the ceremony, and they bought it later that evening, stopped by my house and we did a very simple ceremony on my front porch!

On one occasion, the groom failed to bring the license. The couple had come in town 3 weeks prior from California, and purchased it, but he left at their home. I informed the groom of what needed to take place and he asked me NOT to tell the bride—that he would do that "later."

He failed to give his best man the same instructions. The best man told his wife, who told her sister, who was the aunt of the bride, and when they met for the first time at the Wedding Arbor—IT WAS ON! He was almost breathless as he saw his future wife in her gown. Her father walked her down the aisle. As daddy raised the veil and kissed his little girl goodbye, I could tell by the look on her face that something was wrong.

He took her by the hand—led her to stand before me—and under her breath sternly glared at him and said "I can't believe you forgot the license. The only thing you had to remember to bring was the license. I made the reservations, I brought the rings, I took care of the corsages and boutonnieres, and all you had to do was remember the license and you couldn't even remember that!"

I paused during all this since the only people who could hear it was the three of us and half the wedding party. The best man snickered, and I thought the bride's daggering stare would turn him into a pillar of salt! I began the ceremony—and all seemed to be going quite well until I asked for a moment of silent prayer for one of the grandparents who was no longer with them. In these brief moments of silence—I heard the bride mutter those famous words I wish I had never heard: "I bet you didn't forget the condoms!"

AMEN!

Look Out for the Bees

I really don't envy the wedding photographer. They've got to arrive early, leave late, and above all, capture everything that happens before and after the ceremony. They have to make sure the background is perfect; the gown is in perfect array; the veil hangs "just enough" not to hide the bride's face; make sure the groom's hands are not in his pockets or that he is not chewing gum, keep his attention away from all his buddy's howlings and comments; and has to do it all while being bumped around like a rubber ball.

Most of the time, the bride and groom do not see one another until after the ceremony begins; it's "tradition." Oftentimes today, however, this is not the case. I vividly recall the bride and groom posing in a beautiful wedding garden in late spring. This had to be one of the most beautiful rose gardens I'd ever seen, and for a guy who has never had a green thumb, that's saying a lot. The bride was sitting at an angle on a concrete bench with her head tilted up to see the face of her "soon-to-be." The photographer was doing her best to shoot just the right angle, and all the while being stuck by all the thorns of the rose bushes she was crouching through for the right position. I heard her say, "Okay, smile softly, hold it . . . OH CRAP!"

We laughed because at first we thought she managed to find the "Thorn of all thorns." What she did manage to find were a few bees that were enjoying the flowers surrounding the roses.

With her camera on her neck, battery packs on her belt and extra camera slung under her arm, the girl flew like she was a lightning bug, leaving the bride and groom with a "what do we do now?" look that was priceless!

She stood up, he took off running, and she's screaming "You'd better get you're a* * back over here and help me" The train on her dress was over 15 feet long and she was trapped! He reluctantly returned to help combat the bees. However; sadly enough, he set the stage for the rest of their lives together! Nature at its finest.

From Carli and Brody

"Jimmy Mac,
We love you! At the end of our ceremony you told us three very important things:
#1: There are problems in this world. We are joined as one - deal with the problems as one.
#2: Every morning - wake up and fall in love with each other all over again.
#3: (and the most important) Keep God in the center of our marriage!
The 1-2-3's of marriage are simple - you put them in perspective. Thank you so much - from the bottom of our hearts!"

Ball and Chain

I met the groom—really nice guy (actually thought he was Drew Carey when I saw him from a distance!) He told me he was tired of running from it—it was time—giving up his Man Card—freedom, favorite place on the couch, the whole enchilada!

I cracked up at him because those are some of the jokes I tell the groom (just to get them to relax of course!) He'd been telling his "soon-to-be" bride for the past six months that he was ready to put on the ball and chain. A hearty laugh and off to meet his bride.

As I entered the Bride's Room, I introduced myself and this woman in white charged across the room, laid a bear hug on me that I could have sworn cracked ribs and blurted out "I hear you've got the best sense of humor in the world!"

Catching my breath and wondering what just hit me, I hollered "I used to!"

As she laughed, she turned, reached into her travel bag and pulled out (you guessed it) a ball and chain!

As I stared at it all I could say was "REALLY?"

At the very moment I declared them husband and wife. she was to kiss him as I pulled the ball and chain out of hiding.

We did just that. Not only did he give her a "Second Kiss," he willingly pulled up his pants leg and held his foot steady while I attached it to his ankle. I believe every wedding picture had this in full sight!

Such the happy couple!

"Marriage is an institution,
And I ain't ready for no institution."

—*Mae West*

Bagpipes

I was told there would be bagpipes. They usually make me tear up during funerals. This couple was going to cross the sword, drink wine from the ceremonial cup, and perform as many Scottish rituals as possible during their ceremony.

The bagpiper was outside in the main entrance to the small and cozy chapel. The seating capacity was stated as forty five. There were over sixty in the room, plus two video crews and three photographers. There were five people in the three-man pews. The atmosphere was extremely eclectic ranging from dragons and fairies to statues of saints in the dimly lit room.

The bride entered to the traditional bridal march. The droning from the piper lingered until the stately groom accepted the hand of his bride from her father. The ceremony was exquisite including all the traditions. They kissed—I pronounced them husband and wife, and as they crossed over the sword, the bagpiper had made his way into the already crowded room. He began to play the processional and no one—let me repeat myself—no one had any idea how loud he was until he hit his first note.

Many people, including myself, ducked with the expectation of getting hit by some kind of flying object in the room.

With hands over their ears—many of the well-dressed and overly exuberant attendees cut in front of the wedding couple and made their way out of the chamber door! I was one of the lucky ones—I followed closely behind the bridal couple . . . smiling . . . and going deaf!

Bird Poop

*I*t had to be one of the most beautiful days Las Vegas ever had in the springtime. Everything that could possibly be growing in this garden oasis in the desert was blooming. Trees were filling with leaves and buds—plants had gone from twigs to flowers, and the birds had returned to sing the songs only they could sing.

The groom and I walked to the flowered arch and awaited the rest of the bridal party. He, adorned in full tux including tails, shiny lapels, and not a speck of dust on him anywhere. His hair was meticulously groomed and you could practically see the sky in the shine from his shoes. This guy was dressed to the nines! The music changed and the bridal march began. The bridesmaids were each escorted with a well-dressed groomsman with vest matching their dresses. The palette contained perfectly blended colors that complemented each person and the one they stood beside.

All were in place—the time had come for the bride to begin her journey to this outdoor Shangri-La. The groom looked to his left and then to his right. He rubbed his hands nervously together as the music began—leaned toward me and asked "Can you see her yet, Rev?" As I began to respond, one of those singers who dominated the air flew overhead and left the couple an early present on the shoulder and back of the groom. The best man best identified it as "holy crap!" I reached for my handkerchief and quickly removed the majority of it in one swipe. The groom's eyes were about the size of an American eagle silver dollar when I turned the cloth over—wiped it again and absolutely nothing remained.

I quietly folded it—placed it on the railing behind us and we welcomed the bride. He could say nothing—he marveled at how beautiful his bride was and from that point forward all went according to plan.

At the end of the ceremony, I pronounced them husband and wife. He kissed his bride and I was able to announce them "for the very first time Mr. and Mrs. ____," which is something I am always very proud to do.

Before he walked his bride down the aisle—he released her hand, turned and hugged me and whispered quietly to me: "Thank you so much! She would have killed me!" I just smiled, shook my head and watched them walk away in bliss.

Daddy's Rose

I met with the groom - tall athletic build - handsome guy with a chiseled jaw, perfect teeth, dark hair neatly groomed and a twinkle in his eye for his bride! We spoke and then I left to talk to his future wife who was being traditionally secluded from him. She stopped everything she was doing, requested that everyone leave the room—asked me to sit next to her on the couch in the Bride's Room as she proceeded to tell me about her daddy.

She told me how special he had been in her life and her only prayer was that she wished he could have lived to see this day. He died in a car accident five years earlier and it was his dream to walk her down the aisle and present her hand in marriage. As her eyes filled with tears, I realized they were not tears of sorrow—but tears of pride and adulation for her father. He was a decorated war hero, an awesome husband to her mom and father to all three of his daughters. He was protective and supportive, loving and giving. This beautiful young woman got up from her seat beside me, walked over to a counter and opened a long box. As she removed the white tissue paper, she revealed a beautiful white rose. She asked if I could place this rose on the chair where her father would sit if he were there. I told her I would be honored. I stood and she gave me a hug. She kissed my cheek and whispered "thank you." I left with the rose in my hand, walked out of the room, stood behind the building and cried.

As the wedding began, I stopped at the chair during the opening procession, placed the rose on it and took my place.

The bride's mother walked her beautiful daughter down the aisle and as her mother sat down, she picked up the rose.

I noticed that oftentimes during the ceremony, she would smell it and rub it softly on the side of her face.

I believe her father's spirit lay within that beautiful flower. Sometimes, I have a hard time wrapping my head around what I do and the lives it touches. This one completely grounds me in humility!

"Jimmy -

I was a nervous groom - practically in tears. I had actually thought for a moment to run! Within five minutes of speaking with you, you became a hero, mentor, and father to me. I'll never be able to express how important that was to me at that very moment. My own dad passed away just months before the ceremony and nothing else seemed to matter. He really was watching from heaven and I can't tell you how much it meant for me to shake your hand and get that hug of reassurance. We are so much in love and I'll probably share this moment with her in 20 years!"

Name not published at Groom's request.

Doggie Shakes

Let me set this up for you: one of the most beautifully landscaped golf courses in the Valley! Beautiful lake, the water was still and the sky could not have been a more brilliant blue. The reflection off the water was an artist's canvas—just a few puffy white clouds. The archway for the ceremony stood before some large tannish-brown rocks with flowers abounding on each side. This was going to be the greatest dream scenario for any bride's wedding album! The train on the bride's dress had to have been at least 15 feet long—she completed the portrait for the photographer's dream shots!

If you have a dog and you think it's cute to dress him up in a bow tie and tuxedo collar and let him carry the rings on his back with a pillow tied to him ~ think again! Beautiful wedding—the couple had been living together and had a beautiful two-year-old black lab. He was stocky, wagged his tail and no doubt was happy to see everyone at the wedding.

Escorted by the hand of a six-year-old nephew, the two made their way toward the archway at this beautiful golf course setting with the rings tied to the pillow. The dog's attention was drawn by whistles and calls from the almost 150 guests in attendance.

However, when the mallards flew into the picture and splashed into the water, the dog just seemed to know it was his duty to retrieve them. All 85 pounds of him jerked the lad to the ground and the leash from his hand as the canine leaped onto the rocks and then into the water. The groom was screaming commands as the dog returned to the bank of the lake—without the pillow!

The look on the bride's face was practically criminal as she glared at the groom! Moments later, someone hollered out, "LOOK!" The pillow floated to the top and it was retrieved by one of the groundskeepers. Neatly secured were the two platinum wedding bands still attached with the thin white lace ribbon.

You're probably asking yourself what happened to the dog. He was so happy that he performed his job according to his master's wishes that when he got out of the water, he immediately ran over to the bride's side, shook the muddy water all over the bride and her 20-plus members of the bridal party! I LOVE my job!

The Archbishop of Canterbury

One of the most memorable wedding ceremonies I've performed took place in a very unusual place. A well-known celebrity photographer contacted me and wanted to discuss a wedding ceremony and see if I could do it. We met, I told him "Oh yeah" and before I knew it—I was dressed in full costume as the Archbishop of Canterbury at the end of the Tournament of Kings show at the world famous Excalibur Casino and Hotel here in Las Vegas. His son was coming to Vegas with his bride to get married. They didn't want the "little chapel on the Strip" kind of wedding, but also didn't want a major blow-out either. The dad said he'd take care of all of it. The couple thought they were going to get married in the wedding chapel at the Excalibur—a beautiful location for any bride and groom. However, along with their 25 guests they all attended the evening performance of the magnificent Tournament of Kings. Full regalia including; the Kings on horseback, the jousting, and the Knights of the Round Table as they all perform during a feast while you watch! At the end of the performance, the dad informed them that he had a friend who was going to allow them to lower the round table and have them have their pictures taken on it before they all went to the chapel for the ceremony. As the couple posed for pictures—the lights were dimmed, myself, King Richard, Merlin, and the Court Jester walked across the arena flanked by the Kings on horseback and trumpets sounding our entrance. The bride and groom stood in awe as they realized they were about to get married; right here and right now! I informed them that in order to perform a marriage ceremony the bride would require a bouquet. At that time one of the Kings reached behind his back, rode his steed closer to the bride and presented the flowers to her. The jester had a pillow with rings and with his Majesty's permission; we proceeded with the wedding that has never since been repeated in the arena! It was an amazing night even for me; the newly acclaimed Archbishop of Canterbury!

"*JIMMY MAC - YOU ROCK! Our wedding was a party because of you! I didn't know I could sweat when it was 45° out but I did. You completely made it awesome! Don't know how you managed to calm us down and knock out the nerves - but I know a shrink gets $150 an hour for it! Thanks for everything!* "

— Randy and Rianne

"*This was the moment that Jimmy Mac McNamara broke the ice for us! I will never forget him saying, "Matt - you didn't tell me you were marrying a supermodel!" It made us both relax as you can see.*"

— Matt and Megan

All Gas on Deck

I performed a wedding recently, and it was very cold outside. The wedding garden had a propane heater on the deck that kept the bride's side of the wedding party warm. The groom's mother, a woman of decent size and girth was assisted by a cane. When I asked the audience to "Please rise" as the bride made her way to the altar, the mom wouldn't stand and when someone told her that she needed to stand, she stated that she knew who it was and she was good with sitting down.

The ceremony began. I welcomed everyone, and all seemed to be going well. A few notices of tears in the audience as well as in the eyes of the bride. As I was about to begin the vows, the dear groom's mother felt the need to relieve herself of some bound up gas. There was enough pressure and propulsion to have the entire audience take notice! As a minister, do I dare smile? Do I even pause? As I went for what had hoped would be my last breath, the groom hollered at her "Did ya have to rip one right there in front of the minister and the marriage ceremony?"

The mother looks at him and simply stated "I was just easin' up the pressure!

"The groom looks at his bride and says "Welcome to the family!"

The bride looks at me asks "What should I do?"

I'm not one to holler "RUN GIRL RUN," so I simply made the announcement "Let's all bow our heads and thank the Lord that mama is sitting on the opposite side from the propane heater!"

Once everybody got calmed down from laughing, I continued with the ceremony. I'm still in touch with this couple, and we often laugh about that chilly day.

Grand Canyon

O ne of the challenges of this job is to meet the needs of the wedding couple. In this case—it meant I had to fly to the Grand Canyon. What a thrill! A twenty passenger turbo-prop airplane with the bride and groom and one of my favorite photographers in tow!

We landed and then took an hour and a half four-wheel drive buggy ride down to 700 feet above the Colorado River. The view was spectacular! The bride and groom were searching for a location that was best suited for the background for their wedding pictures. They had flown 15 hours to get to Las Vegas (wonderful overseas couple), and wanted to be certain that their pictures would be no less than perfect.

They found their ideal location and had the heels of their boots barely 18 inches from the edge of the 700 foot cliff! I let them know they could still get the same effect by standing three to five feet away from the cliff.

"We're good Jimmy . . . let's do this!" It was THEN that I thanked God for their feet being a foot and a half away and not mine! (I also thanked Him for the fact that I had gotten paid in advance for my services!) I believe the gusty winds unnerved them a bit—but all went well and it was a memorable day!

Granny's Gone Wild!

I was preparing to marry a couple who met on a social media network. They talked back and forth via the internet for several months and finally decided they needed to meet face to face. By this time, they knew one another (as well as all the friends and things that they had in common), and having fallen in love decided to tie the knot. I got the opportunity to meet with the two of them for coffee about a month prior to their ceremony. They were a fun couple, full of life and loved doing things outdoors together—which is why they chose an outdoor venue for their wedding. They also wanted to remember how they met one another so they chose something a little bit different at the end of their ceremony.

Here's the day—groom in a black tux with the most vivid turquoise blue vest I'd ever seen and three men standing by his side. Bridesmaids walk the aisle with the same blue on their gowns, and once in the picture, it was a beautiful sight! Enter the bride—form-fitting white dress that wrapped her elegantly! The ceremony begins without a dry eye in the house.

Even the groom's grandmother sitting on the front row with her cane removed a white lace hankie and gently patted her eyes—such a sweet and gentle air about her.

The time arrived for those hallowed words, "By the power vested in me by the State of Nevada, in the witness of family and friends, and in the presence of God, I now pronounce you husband and wife. You may kiss your bride." They shared their first kiss as a married couple.

They held hands, gazing into one another's eyes as I made the next pronouncement at their request "You may now update your Facebook status," at which time they both pulled out their cell phones and made the changes.

Everyone laughed. Well . . . almost everyone! As the married couple walked down the aisle, the sweet grandmother on the front row turned into a scorned Granny from the Beverly Hillbillies. With her cane pointed at my face, she charged me saying "YOU THINK THAT WAS FUNNY? IS THAT IN THE BIBLE?" The groom's father was still laughing when he saw his mom in a rage. He tried to calm her down saying that was what they had requested. I escaped with my life and they escaped with some pretty awesome pictures of "Granny Gone Wild!"

Things Overheard by Family and Friends

- "She looks beautiful!"
- "She looks amazing!"
- "My daughter looks like a princess."
- "I heard she was pregnant"
- "Her dress cost over $2K and she's wearing sneakers."
- "I saw her dress ... white ... REALLY?"
- "We bought a disposable camera for tonight"
- "I deserved him—not her."
- "Her daddy doesn't know."
- "It's not too late to run, son."
- "We got so drunk last night ... "
- "Her dress is so tight that she coughed and one of her boobs popped out in the dressing room."
- "All the bridesmaids look like hoochie mamas"

- "She covered THAT tattoo with makeup"
- "She threw up, but it missed her dress."
- "I can't believe he rented a tux."
- "I believe I died and went to Fashionista Hell."
- "It would have been cheaper to do this back home."
- "This is her first and his fourth."
- "Hey preacher—you married?"

We're Gonna Have Kids!

I performed a wedding for what I believe was my oldest couple yet. She was 68 and he was 72. They were as cute as they could be. They had been living together for over 18 years and decided to finally make it legal. I was curious, and asked them why they waited so long to get married. They looked into one another's eyes for a moment, simultaneously turned their heads toward me and said "We decided we wanted to have kids!"

"Hi Jim,

I truly believe that some things happen for a reason, like meeting a future spouse, or meeting a person that comes along at just the right time. By accident? I don't think so. We feel blessed that you were part of our day, really enjoyed meeting you, and are very happy that the other two guys were booked for our day!!! Too bad you are in such high demand and couldn't stay for lunch - a good time was had! Ben's daughter Amanda is going to get married in the fall... we are trying to talk her into doing it in Henderson, and that would give us a reason to give you a call. Thanks again and hopefully the rest of the day went well for you."

—Ben & Kathy

Motorcycle Mama

I love telling my brides and grooms something cheesy once in a while. One of them is a terrific line taken from a famous fast food restaurant chain. "Have it your way!" It's the only time they're ever going to do this again in their lives so they should make it what they want it to be.

I had been emailing back and forth for several months with a bride from Canada concerning her special day. They had planned to have a '50s-themed wedding and wanted to know if I had any suggestions on what could be done.

Huh? Me have some suggestions? I laughed and asked her how she would like it if Pastor Fonzie himself brought her out on his motorcycle. She must have screamed when she read the email. Fast forward to the day of the wedding. It was staged in a beautiful orchard area of one of my favorite wedding gardens. The bride is behind the main building and completely out of sight from the audience who has absolutely no idea that she will be arriving on the back of a motorcycle. I was dressed in leather hat, jacket, and jeans. The bride climbed on after being cautioned that she needed to avoid the exhaust pipes because they get hot quickly and will damage her dress.

She heard, but the dress didn't. Although not very noticeable—it will be a keepsake with special memories later. As we approached the final turn toward the orchard, there were some very upset attendees who thought it was just wrong to have someone on a motorcycle rev their engine and sound their horn just as a wedding was about to start, and a posse started to form!

Once they saw the bride on the back of the motorcycle, they all stood cheering! I drove forward to her father who was waiting to walk her down the aisle.

I've since ridden one other precious bride on the back of my motorcycle, who is my world-famous hairstylist and dear friend. I love my job and the very special people I get to meet and whose lives touch mine as well.

Lollipop Rings

*I*t was a spring wedding; a bit warm for April in Las Vegas, but beautiful nonetheless. There were only seven people in the bridal party, and it was one of those "let's choose a venue when we get there" kind of weddings that are becoming quite popular in this city. The couple gets in town a day early, visits local scenery and then chooses where they'd like to get married. I've performed weddings in parking lots, golf courses, at the "Welcome to Las Vegas" sign and even on the sidewalk in front of many of the beautiful and lavish buildings, fountains and gardens.

This couple was pretty cool—he wore dress slacks, a dress shirt with no tie and a sport coat; she wore a white knee-length dress and carried a white rose held close to her. There was no doubt she was a bride, and the smile on her face proved it! Two more people with cameras appeared and we were off!

We stopped at one of the most beautiful and world-famous water features in Las Vegas and they decided "this was the place."

With everyone in place and the license signed, I began the brief ceremony. When I asked for the rings, I thought the best man was joking as many do. I usually get the "where did they go?" routine' but this one must have left a very surprised look on my face. As he handed it to the groom who proceeded to place it on the bride's finger,I inadvertently asked "Are you serious?"   They both laughed and nodded "Yes."

No law says you can't so they took their Lollipop rings and exchanged them, repeating their vows and looking as serious as any couple I've ever married.

After the ceremony, they apologized and said they should have given me the heads-up—but the custom rings they had ordered did not make it before they left home for the trip, so they were going to seal these in a glass container and keep it with their wedding picture when they returned home. We all had a good laugh, and I still ask myself to this day if they hadn't told me just to see the look on my face! It just goes to show that even I can get surprised in this business.

"Hello Jimmy Mac! It was so great to have you be our minister for our wedding. You were fabulous. I only wish we were able to have gotten to know you better and vice versa. But you really did just fit right in and worked so well with our family. That is God at work, isn't it? We had no fear, no worries, just trust it would all work out and come together perfectly. And it so did. So, thank you for being willing and able.

We knew that our vows to each other in front of the audience was going to be what we wanted, and you providing the overall message and making it official and so right on was perfect. We appreciated what you had to share and add to the rest of the evening.

And, I did take a look at your website. What an incredible message you have to share and what a beautiful wife you have, as you know very well. I can see the strength and power you both bring to so many people. It's a beautiful thing. I love it. Like I mentioned, we should certainly get together again very soon."

—Dave and Brooke

Riding into the Sunset

There are times I almost feel guilty for charging for some of these weddings. (But believe me—I get over it quickly!) I've performed a dozen or so weddings on horseback. That's right, the wedding couple and I are all on horses—we ride to a beautiful setting and they're side by side while I perform the ceremony. I walk around and hand each one their rings as they repeat their vows.

Most of the time, everything goes according to plan. The ranch who sells these packages has very docile horses. Most of the people who choose these venues are not skilled riders, and for the most part, don't need to be. However, there are times when the horses recognize a familiar bridle path and know they're supposed to be walking down it. Therefore one must know the use of the reins and hold the horse in place. I had one groom whose horse decided "all this is nice—but I gotta go" and proceeded to do just that. The bride was an experienced rider and quickly corralled the two of them back to the original wedding spot. The groom, a slightly embarrassed British chap knew he was marrying an equestrian and although he was a bit red in the face, nonetheless continued with the ceremony. The horse was not the least bit pleased.

As the vows began—his trusty steed felt the need to relieve himself with enough gas to choke all of us. The bride's horse seemed to take this personally and during her vows relieved himself of at least a gallon of retained fluids!

All the while, my poor horse was suffering from what appeared to be irritable bowel syndrome and through the tears of all the laughter, as I pronounced them husband and wife, mine let go of about a week's saved up manure in a good ten second drop!

They rode off into the sunset as I turned my horse around to a safe and clean distance to dismount. There's just something about the great outdoors.

How Did You Meet?

- "We met at church. It was love at first sight. We both had to wait until we were divorced before we could start dating."

- "We met in a bar. It was deer season—me and some guys came in and she was the bartender. I asked her if she hunted—she nodded—we went out for a few beers and went bowling. That was two months ago and here we are."

- "We met hiking one time with friends. Been walking the same path ever since."

- "We're both in the Air Force. We met on deployment."

- "We met during a 5k run. I passed him sitting on the curb—went back and jogged in place asking him if he was alright. He said he had a blister—I called him a sissy and he's been chasing me ever since."

* "I saw her in the waiting room of my office. I did a root canal on her. Oh yeah, I'm her dentist too."

* "I saw him in the grocery store and noticed he didn't buy any feminine hygiene products or TV dinners. I took it that he wasn't married and he could cook."

* "We've known each other since we were kids in grade school. We both married other people and went our separate ways. We saw each other again at our 20th high school reunion and were both single again. It started from there."

* "We met on Facebook."

- "Her sister dated my brother. Then he dated her and then her sister again. He said I could have her."

- "We met in a bank. I was a teller and he was a large depositor."

- "I'm a waitress. He'd come in a couple of times a week to the restaurant. He'd order the same food over and over—I figured he'd be easy to cook for so I asked him out."

- "I met him at night school. He worked a full time job and was trying to get ahead in life. I admired that in him."

Cold Renewal

O n occasion a couple will step up and renew their vows. Oftentimes it's at a designated anniversary (10th, 20th, etc.). This wonderful couple was from overseas and celebrating their 50th wedding anniversary. Absolutely beautiful couple but being islanders, the December temperatures were a bit cold on them. There was a heater on one side of the seating area and they opted for me to perform the ceremony under the canopy of the heater.

The bride was dressed in traditional clothing while the husband was in a comfortable jacket and tie. Both of them, well into their 70's, were a very cute and loving couple. The groom was very cold, but his loving wife stood very stoic and smiling—staring into his eyes the entire time. It was very touching, until I began the vows. I turned to him and said "Would you take this woman all over again, to be your lawfully wedded wife?"

His response: "Sure."

Her smile changed to one of scolding.

Bride: "What do you mean, 'Sure'? You're supposed to say 'I do.' . . . Now, say it!"

Groom: "Would it mean we get inside sooner? Okay, then, I DO!"

The fun never ends!

Jackhammer Tears

*H*ave I mentioned that I love my job? I get to see young (and not so young) couples commit themselves to one another for the rest of their lives. The younger ones need some help along the way. Rarely do they ask for marital advice—they just want to make it through the wedding without crying, stuttering, or embarrassing themselves and that's mostly from the groom!

I even had one young guy offer me $20 if I could keep him from crying. I try to keep everything light-hearted just for that reason. I tell the groom that it's okay to "tear up a bit, that chicks dig tears." I almost always say it to him in front of the members of his wedding party so everyone gets to keep it fun. But I also add "But if you start bawlin' like a three-year-old little girl, I'm gonna tap my book like this (fingers on back of book.) What this is gonna do is distract you and at the same time, it's gonna be the signal for your best man to get your Man Card outta yer pocket and hold it for the first 90 days of your marriage!" It usually works out pretty well and we're off to begin a great wedding! But in this particular case, all the groom had to do was see the wedding party and especially his daddy on the front row and it was on!

He cried so hard that his shoulders practically hit his ears! Somebody even said he resembled a human jack hammer! At that point, I had people hollering at me "Don't tap the book . . . HIT HIM WITH IT!"

We got through the wedding and all ended well.

There are some ceremonies you just don't forget!

Lost Ring and Flames

You ever just have "one of those days?" This was one of them. Four weddings completed—one more to finish off the day.

The first one had a baby that just did not want to be there and cried the entire ceremony. The second one forgot their license and had plans of leaving right after the service for Hawaii and felt the need to argue that I was being unreasonable. (Note to all: It ain't legal 'til I do the paperwork!) The third one was good—great couple—happy, in love, left a generous tip too! The fourth one was interesting—the daddy really didn't want to release his daughter's hand over to the groom and I mean literally did not want his daughter marrying this guy. He ended up leaving his daughter there and left not to be seen again by the wedding party. The bride didn't seem bothered by his absence either.

Here comes the fifth one. "Dear Lord—please make it a good one!" The groom was a fun-loving and happy-go-lucky guy. It was apparent that he and his buddies had been drinking the better part of the day. We talked, completed the required paperwork, and I went to visit with the bride.

A beautiful girl who was ready to take on the happiest day of her life! I introduced myself to her and she gave me a hug and said she'd been to my website and was just happy I was performing the ceremony. Those kind words helped relieve the stress of the earlier part of my day. Her words echoed in my mind "Nothing can ruin this day for me today!"

The ceremony began—it was flawless! All the guys were well-behaved in the wedding party.

There was a table set behind us with the Unity Candle ceremony waiting in the balance. It came time for the best man to hand the groom the bride's ring.

Between his shaking hand and the groom scared to death he was going to "mess sumthin' up"—the ring left his hand, rolled down the bride's gown, and ever so carefully . . . fell between the deck boards of this beautiful outdoor gazebo which stood partially over the reflection pond. I reached to try and catch it as did the bride and groom with no success. With the three of us crouched down—the bride quickly took off her engagement ring and whispered "Use this" and handed it to the groom. We all stood up—the bride was laughing and we continued. No one was the smarter (or so we thought.)

We continued with the ceremony and as we were about to step back to begin the candle ceremony, one of the young men who had been a part of the guys' party had stripped down to his boxer shorts and socks and stated "I'll go get it!" I looked at him and hollered "The water is seven inches deep—just get dressed!"

All the cameras were pointing in his direction—the laughter was overwhelming! We continued to the table and the bride4 and groom lit their tapers, and with the proper reading, together lit the main candle. As they began to walk away from the candle and the arbor, the bride turned to see if the self-appointed "Ring Recoverer" had gotten dressed, As she did, her veil brushed across the large candle and immediately ignited. I put one of my hands above the flame and pulled it down across the molten nylon. The flame was extinguished, and the only ones who knew it were the bridesmaid and the groom.

The bridesmaid removed the veil very discreetly, and I pronounced the couple husband and wife. As they walked away she asked me if I was alright. My hand was sealed shut with the smell of burning plastic, and we just smiled as a catastrophe had been avoided.

One of the groundskeepers came with a screw gun, removed the board, and the ring was recovered during the photographer's session. I walked over, placed the ring in the groom's hand, who in turn, placed it on his wife's finger. They kissed again, and all was well.

And everyone thinks all we do is just get people to say "I do."

Cell Phone Won't Float

A couple of years ago I was performing a wedding at a beautiful wedding garden here in Las Vegas. The bride was less than two breaths away from being a celebrity on a certain "monster show" for women in her position! I managed to get her calmed down before the ceremony, and little did I know that she was marrying a man of few words.

They each had written their own vows and when it came time to recite them, he simply stated "I love you. I want you to have my babies. If you'll keep the trailer clean, I'll keep food in it and we can fish on the weekends."

Doing my best not to make any facial changes either way, I put the microphone in front of her. She proceeded for the next ten minutes to thank God, His mother, all the Saints (by name no less) fairies, butterflies, fireflies, all kinds of flies; and about halfway into her vows, the groom's cell phone rang. He was quick to cancel the call.

Her eyes were about to roll back into her head. I was expecting to see her head rotate a full 360° so I calmly put my hand on her forearm and smiled at her. "It's okay, sweetie . . . just continue."

When she completed her vows, I pronounced them husband and wife. They kissed and I followed them over for a final congratulations. During their walk over to the reflection pond, she reached her hand into his pocket and retrieved his cell phone. Just when you thought things couldn't have gotten worse: "Isn't this your ex-girlfriend?" the bride exclaimed!

One would think he would have remembered to at least delete her picture before he got married!

Believe me, I think if Stephen King got wind of it he could have written an entire novel on this one. That was the day I learned to moonwalk! Feet get me outta there!

INTERESTING FACT: Did you know if done properly, an iPhone can skip twice on water before sinking to the bottom?

Pink Socks

S ometimes you just gotta "go with the flow." I'd been in contact with this particular bride and groom for a few months and we actually became good friends on the phone and through all the emails. We had this ceremony down pat!

I visited with the bride for the first time, and there were hugs and laughter and a few shattered nerves, but she was good to go and really excited! I went next door to the infamous "Groom Room" where you never know what to expect. There were seven guys and a groom—all about to finish getting dressed and passing around flasks that were filled with a familiar scent that only Jose Cuervo could create! To say the least, they appeared to be very happy. They'd known one another since elementary school—all grew up on the same street—and this guy was the last one of the bunch to get married. He was 27 and said it was "time for him to get whipped like the rest of them." It was the best camaraderie I'd seen in many years!

The groom looked at me and said "We're all in! We've stood beside one another for a couple of decades! Hey Pastor . . . are you in?" I looked at him and proudly stated "Im in!"

They all raised their pants to expose—pink socks! I laughed and said "If I had known—I would have worn mine."

Much to my surprise the groom reaches in the bag and said "We knew you were one of us, here's yours!" He handed me a pair of the loudest pair of fuchsia socks I'd ever seen. And he just stood there— smiling. And I put them on!

Before I pronounced them husband and wife—I mentioned that each of these guys had known one another since the first grade and they've remained friends all these years supporting one another and to show their solidarity—they've done this; at which time they all raised their pants legs exposing the infamous colored socks. People were standing up with their cameras—at which time the bride shook her head and said "Jimmy—you don't have any?"

I raised my pants legs and she laughed—gave me a hug and a kiss on the cheek and then ... kissed her new husband.

Who would have ever thought I'd have gotten a kiss before the groom!

"Jimmy,

How fun you were to officiate our wedding in Las Vegas. We're back home in England now, but we'll never forget how absolutely wonderful it was to have you on horseback with us when we wed. When we visit the States again next year, we'd love to visit with you again and perhaps take you and your missus to dinner."

—Craig and Sharon

To The Dry Cleaners Now!

*T*here are those who put the proverbial "cart before the horse," and I have officiated numerous weddings where the couple already has a child. In this one memorable occasion, both had children from a previous marriage; a total of three smaller kids plus an infant under a year old together.

They were all dressed in formal attire including the newest member. The other three were all under the age of six and required a lot of attention. The groom carried the baby and when it came time to exchange vows and rings, no one stepped up to hold the baby during this romantic and special time. I, being the accommodating one, took the baby while they did this. I'll never forget the look on this precious baby's face when he smiled . . . and unloaded on me! As if the full diaper wasn't enough, he managed to let go of what seemed like two quarts of the worst smelling baby formula imaginable! I quickly handed him back to the embarrassed couple when the bride said,

"I think it's time we get him off breast milk!" I really did not want to hear that!

Very thankful it was my last wedding of the day. First stop on the way home ... the dry cleaners!

Gymnastics by Mistake

I know it's the "in" style and all the young ladies feel the need to wear them. High heels today are tall, shiny, lots of "armor" on them and the colors are as many as the rainbow. However, if you've never worn them in public, please practice before you do!

The bridesmaids were all dressed in dark red (don't get me to lying about the shade of red; to this country boy, it was just a dark red.) The dresses were fairly short for a wedding and very snug fitting. When approaching the gazebo where the wedding was taking place, one of the ladies slightly slipped on the small inclined ramp. She caught her balance, laughed and continued her walk to the front. It was a typical hot Las Vegas summer day and what began as a "sweat-fest" waiting for the bridal party to arrive, was almost a welcomed moment of levity. One person even commented "Did anyone get that on video?" An affirmative response was made and everyone laughed.

The next who was due in line was the bridesmaid. However, because the ring bearer and flower girl were so young, they came next. The ring bearer could not have been more than three years old and sporting his "mini-tux" he was as cute as he could be!

The flower girl was an adorable child, probably five years old or so and she was meticulous in being certain to drop just the right amount of fresh rose petals along the route for the bride. As they were scurried to their assigned positions on either side of the wedding party, the bridesmaid made her entrance being cautious not to step on any of the flowered path.

As she turned the corner to make her final approach, everyone could tell she had never worn shoes that tall before! The platform appeared to be well over an inch tall and the heels were pushing at least six inches. It was as though her feet were two feet in front of her at all times.

Everyone smiled a cautious smile as she made her way up the ramp, and just as this story builds up to the very moment you all expected . . . she made it! She approached the archway overly-confident and that's when it happened; she slipped on a rose petal.

Not only did she fall—but she fell forward on those mega-heels and did a complete somersault. The groom and I took her hands and caught her from falling backwards. The red on her face bore her embarrassment, but when she stood up and gained her composure, assuring everyone she was not hurt, the only comment she could make was "Sure am glad I decided to wear underwear today!"

So was I.

From Russia With Love

I try to meet each and every bride and groom before each wedding ceremony. The groom brought in the license and had a friend who was going to sign as the witness. As grooms go, he wasn't a "Prince Charming" by any standards of GQ Magazine, but was really excited about getting married. I spoke briefly with him and there was little time available to meet with the bride. I did notice that her name was of Russian descent, and he confirmed the proper pronunciation so as not to embarrass anyone.

We took our places and as the bride made her way forward, I was taken aback by the stature and beauty of this woman. First notice was of the wedding dress. It was more like a white party dress—no back, no shoulders. It was cut low and cut high, if you know what I mean. Her hair and make-up were ready for the cover of any high fashion magazine! She walked unescorted and as I asked them to face one another, she also had a question for me.

In a thick Russian accent, she asked of me "Are you single, Pastor?"

I immediately told her "no."

Her response: "Too bad. Please continue!"

I know what you're thinking, but I'd just like to believe she wasn't looking for a free ticket into the country.

They were in LOVE!

It's All About the Hair

Oftentimes the wedding party is standing anxiously awaiting the appearance of the bride. When the traditional song is played all eyes are at the back of the chapel looking for the first glimpse of the beautiful woman in her gown. In this one instance—the anticipation lasted almost a full twenty minutes. All eyes shifted from the rear of the church to the bridesmaid who spoke aloud "She is just putting the finishing touches on her hair." At one point one of the ushers went to see if the bride was still at the location . . . thinking she may have changed her mind.

The moment had arrived—the music began to play and the rear doors opened. There stood this magnificent bride, ethereal in appearance. The groom leaned over and whispered to me "She looks like an angel just came down to earth!" I must admit she was beautiful. Her make-up was barely visible through the lace veil which covered her face. The low cut on the front of the gown made her slender neck appear even more elegant than when I had met her a week prior. Her hair was meticulous—every golden lock perfectly placed. She was a portrait waiting to be painted. Exquisite!

Her father escorted her down the aisle—short strides in his step and beaming with pride.

His head turned from left to right accepting the nods of adulation and admiration for his youngest daughter. The two stopped as I welcomed everyone to the ceremony.

"Who presents this woman's hand in marriage?" I asked.

"I, my wife, and my family," the father announced with the voice of a professional speaker. He lifted the veil to kiss his daughter goodbye, and I could see the tears swell in his eyes. This tender moment between the bride and her father lapsed quickly.

At the same time as he raised the veil, his cuff link caught the one bobby pin that was holding all her curls in place. In one brief moment, the bride's hair fell like a wet mop. The hair and veil both got caught on the father's cuff, and as the nervous patriarch attempted to move, many of the curls which by this time had proven to be "add-ons" left with him. He had as much hair on his arm as the bride had remaining on her head. The bride stood there staring at her father. His face was filled with remorse, and she felt so badly she simply said "I love you, Daddy!" He kissed her with tears running down his face.

She stepped in front of me looking into her soon-to-be husband's eyes and asked "So what have you and Jimmy been doing for the past half-hour?" We all laughed and continued with the ceremony. She was grateful that they had hired two wedding photographers since there was one outside with the wedding party and one had been assigned to her during her preparation time.

But I have to be honest with ya'll . . . for just a fleeting moment I believe my heart stopped that day!

From the Mouths of Babes

I have performed many wedding ceremonies where the couple has been previously married and have had kids. Having those children take an active part in the ceremony is becoming a tradition and is being recognized as a huge part of acceptance by both the bride and groom. The children can feel the warmth and importance when they take part in the ceremony and even part of a Sand Ceremony as well.

Take the case of a young four-year-old who we'll call Bobby. Bobby was dressed in a full tux—vest—cummerbund, and his bright red bowtie stood out against his dark brown eyes and black hair. Standing about three feet tall, he stood out in the wedding party. He stood beside the groom as the best man and made his "mommy bride" so very proud. She shed tears as she approached the altar just looking at her favorite two men!

When performing the ceremony, Bobby stood proud—never said a word and looked admirably at his mom and future dad.

When it came time to ask for the rings, I spoke into the microphone and asked, "Bobby, do you have the wedding ring for your mommy?" At this time, Bobby was going to say into the microphone, "Yes sir, here is the ring for the bride," just as we had rehearsed. Simple enough—right? When I placed the microphone in front of Bobby's mouth—his words rang as clear as a bell on a sunny day "MY MOMMY'S GONNA HAVE A BABY!" The look on everyone's face was a definite "Kodak Moment!"

Bobby just smiled and handed the ring as if nothing had ever happened. The bride had gone from red-faced to pale and back to red. Bobby stood proud waiting for his next line. With heads shaking in disbelief, I asked the wedding couple if they wanted me to hold the mic in front of him again when I asked for the groom's ring.

The bride's comment "What could it hurt now?" hung in the air for just a moment before the groom exclaimed "NO! He walked in on us doing it." It was then the groom realized the microphone was in front of his mouth.

At this very instant, little Bobby had been vindicated!

The Groom's Mom

We all understand the love between the bride and her daddy; especially if she is either the youngest or only daughter getting married. Daddy's can be very protective or as some would say, "Gotta keep my baby girl shotgun safe!"

But let's not forget the groom's mother. If he is the youngest or the only son, a mother's love can be just as protective, if not overbearing. Take the case of one mom who insisted that she be the one to walk her son down the aisle to their own song. She even handmade his boutonniere.

Mom actually stepped up to him as he stood waiting on his bride; licked her hankie and wiped some lipstick off his cheek—all the time asking why the girl is making her son wait. As I looked out among the small wedding party, eyebrows were raised and a look of disbelief came over many of the faces of the well-wishers. Nevertheless, the ceremony continued as the bride entered unescorted down the aisle. I had the groom meet her at the back of the audience, and I could hear the mother say in a low muffled voice "She couldn't find the altar on her own?"

By this time, people were looking toward me for some kind of resolve. I continued and not another sound was made by the anxious mom until the bride repeated her vows. I have put her comments in parenthesis as they were made while the bride spoke:

"I promise to you John before our family and friends to commit my love to you," (you'd better) "to respect you," (you sure better) "to be with you through life's changes" (uh-huh!) "and to nurture and strengthen the love between us as long as we both shall live" (or I'll be over there!) The groom hung his head when the bride asked "Am I marrying you or her?"

You could hear a pin drop as the ceremony continued. I'd like to be able to tell you that the look on the mom's face was priceless—but to be honest with you, I never raised my head back up until I pronounced them husband and wife. By this time, the bride laid a kiss on the groom that would have made a sailor blush! She had both arms wrapped around his as they walked their recessional toward the photographers for pictures. The woman's eyes locked onto mine. As she walked over and thanked me for a beautiful ceremony, I noticed the tears in her eyes and almost felt sorry for her. I smiled and said "Sooner or later, they all leave the nest." A grin broke across her face as she said "Oh no—they're going to live with me for a year until he finishes his graduate school."

Heaven help them all!

Gung-Ho Bride

I love to hear that the wedding couple is especially happy on their wedding day. There is usually a lot of stressed nerves and oftentimes some anxious moments from either one or the other and sometimes both. This wedding was different.

The groom was calm and collected—shook my hand so hard I thought he was going to retain a couple of the fingers for souvenirs. He had a witness with him to sign the marriage license and his only question was "When do we do this?"

I smiled and told him we were waiting on the wedding planner's signal to "Go!" However, we were still 30 minutes early and all the guests had not yet arrived so "just relax and go visit with some of your friends." He walked out at a very brisk pace and began to socialize with family members.

I walked over to the bride's room and met the happiest bride I'd ever met! She was smiling and laughing and when I introduced myself, she ran up to me and gave me a rib-crushing hug. She said she was soooo ready to get married! Her over-exuberance was contagious. Others in the room were becoming infected with her happiness.

The bridesmaids were "high-fiving" one another and even swatting one another on the rear ends saying things like "Great job on the hair!" and "love the necklace, babe" as if they were all NFL players.

I asked the bride if she had any questions and her response was "When do we roll?"

I glanced at my watch, smiled and informed her that we were still a good 20 minutes away from the starting time.

I thought I was witnessing the largest sugar rush from any group of human beings on the planet!

Fast forward to the ceremony—it was all I could to get the groom to slow down his walk to the altar with me. I explained to him that the photographer needed time to reposition himself.

He agreed and when we arrived, he stood there beaming.

The rest of the wedding party arrived—each more excited than the one before. Even the little flower girl who was dropping rose petals in preparation of the bride's arrival was almost in a dead run.

The music began and the bride was in sight. Her father was escorting her down the path. It was apparent he actually had to hold her back as she was at least a full step ahead of him.

My question of "Who gives this woman's hand in marriage" was given a hasty response "Her family and I— here . . . take her!"

The laughter subsided as the groom took her hand, brought her to stand before me, and she immediately began to giggle and eventually broke out into laughter.

"Forget all this," she stated . . . "I DO!"

"So do I," was his response. They lunged forward and kissed.

I quickly responded in a quiet whisper "We'll do the legal part after the pictures." They took one another by the arm and walked away laughing and hugging.

I guess they really wanted to get married!

Things Overheard by the Bride and Groom

Bride to Groom:

- "I'm wearing the thong you bought me."
- "My boobs are killing me!"
- "Mom is acting like a royal bee-yatch!"
- "I just felt the baby kick."
- "I just ripped a silent one."
- "I didn't know you could clean up this good!"
- "Did you take out the piercing?"
- "Dad found out"
- "I keep popping out of this dress!"
- "You look more handsome today than ever!"
- "I started today"

Groom to bride:

- "The way you look is how I will always remember you."

- "You look so—so—HOT!"
- "You're beautiful." (Crying like a baby.)
- "Your cousin looks like a slut"
- "Your dad is drunk"
- "My mom is loaded"
- "I'm commando!"
- "This tux is giving me a wedgie"
- "I can see up your dress with these rented shoes."
- "I think you dad is trying to hook up with my aunt!"
- "I think I just peed myself just a little bit."

"Let's Play a Joke on Him"

Oftentimes the best way to relieve the nerves of the bride or groom is to get them to laugh. I've been told I've got a gift in this department. I was speaking to a very nervous bride who was sharing with me and her bridesmaid that her fiancé let's nothing bother him, and he was probably "laughing his butt" off at that very moment while she was shaking and ready to cry.

Feeling the imbalance of what she thought was wrong, I asked her if she'd like to have a little fun with him.

"Whatcha got in mind preacher?"

I told her that since we were using the standard vows, I could always begin by saying, "Before the ceremony, I visited with the bride and she informed me that the couple has written their own vows, so let's begin with the groom."

She practically screamed "YES! YES! Let's nail him to the wall!"

She and her wedding party were ready to pound this poor boy into the floor—she seemed to have liked it too much . . . way too much!

I went and met with the groom—great guy— and it was apparent that BOTH of these kids had great senses of humor. So I shared the "secret" with him.

He looked at me and asked "Have you got something I can read? Let's turn this whole thing around!" I love a good challenge. I printed him out a small piece of paper that appeared to be some notes and it was "on!"

When it came time for the vows, I made the announcement, and she just smiled really big waiting for the shocked look on his face.

Her eyes began to get bigger and bigger as he pulled out the "vows he had written" and began to read them.

His sincerity was overflowing and I could hear her quietly whisper "Seriously—you really wrote them?"

As I turned to her and held the microphone in front of her, she looked at him—she looked at me—and stated "I know where *this* came from—give me that mic!" In an instant she declared her love for him, her desire to spend the rest of her life with him, and vowed to always have that same sense of spontaneity and fun with one another!

I took a moment to explain it to the audience, who was a bit surprised at the actions, but laughing nonetheless.

I can see many years of smiles between these two!

Belly Bump

*N*ope—not what you're thinking, but it would have made a lot more sense than this one.

The groom was tall—probably a good 6'4" with an athletic build. There was no doubt this guy spent a good amount of time outdoors. He sported a great tan and the sun had bleached his spiked hair that left a very West Coast feel about him. The term "surfer dude" would have fit him to a tee!

This was one of those rare occasions in which I was unable to meet with the bride prior to the ceremony. She had arrived late at the wedding garden and had yet to put on her gown. Rumor had it she spent most of the day in makeup and hair appointments. I would have to get all my information from the groom for the ceremony; something that could prove to be a bit dangerous if not downright suicidal for a minister!

The info obtained seemed safe—nothing other than the usual; where and how they met, things in common, both enjoyed outdoor sports like kayaking, sand volleyball and the like.

They were also very competitive as a team—racing and playing against others. They appeared to be a couple with a lot in common.

The time came for the bride to walk down the aisle. She was as tall as her stately father. She was also about to marry a man as tall as herself. At 5'10" I felt dwarfed! They looked eye to eye standing as statuesque as any I've ever had the honor to wed. The rings were also the largest I'd ever seen as well.

When I pronounced them husband and wife they engaged in a full-on kiss that seemed to last as long as a buffet line in any casino in Las Vegas!

After the kiss they did something I thought I would never again see (nor have I!)

They leaned back and thrust their bellies toward one another until they seemed to have crashed into one another. They also followed this up with a "high five!" I just wondered if I should declare them "Husband and wife" . . . or the champions!

"Yer Gonna Snip What?"

*T*his is a classic case of the best man conspiring with the bride in an elaborate plot to mess with the groom's head. And I do mean classic.

Take one playful bride—ready to marry the love of her life in a ceremony to be remembered by all. She was non-practicing in her religion and told her fiancé that she wanted to begin attending Temple soon after they were married. The only problem was that the church leader not only refused to do the ceremony, but would not allow them into Temple unless he, the groom, first completed the lessons and follow the traditional circumcision during the wedding ceremony. His attempts to convince her that the circumcision that was performed on him as an infant should suffice—but the bride explained that someone who was trained in the ways of the old testament had to do an additional "snip" to complete the ceremonial promise and tradition. Enter Jimmy Mac!

Now I'll be honest, I hate to lie to anyone, but in this case I found it more to be acting rather than lying. The groom met with me in private and appeared a bit nervous, to say the least.

He asked me about the procedure, and I let him know it's not a procedure—it's a religious tradition thousands of years old. I also allowed him to think that I've done this many times in the past and "it consists of a very tiny cut that most of the time doesn't even bleed."

He questioned privacy and I let him know that it takes place just after the vows and that a table would be in place behind us. His back would be to the congregation and would be witnessed only by the bride and the best man.

This still was apparently not enough to calm him, but I did let him know that I would be wearing gloves and that everything was already on the table under a white linen cloth and it was sterile. As I was speaking with him, I could hear snickering outside the door as a small entourage of friends tried to listen in on our private conversation. It was all I could do to keep a straight face.

The time had come—he and I walked side by side up the aisle and his focus was on nothing more than the table and the contents on top of it. He continued to look over his shoulder as the bridal party made their way and took their places.

What he didn't realize was that the entire congregation was in on the joke. The bride made her way to the altar escorted by her father who proudly recognized those who were giving him kudos along the way. For just a brief fleeting moment, the groom's eyes locked onto his brides and all thoughts of religious surgery seemed to be a galaxy away.

"Who gives this woman's hand in marriage?" I asked.

"Her mother, our family, and I," responded the proud father.

I nudged the groom to take her hand and bring her back to stand before me.

As I asked the Maid of Honor to hold the bride's bouquet, the all-so-playful bride whispered gently "Are you ready to become the man I've always wanted?" That poor guy swallowed so loudly, I thought the first row of people sitting six feet away could hear it. He forced a smile and the ceremony proceeded. All went well including the vows, which they both repeated with a strong voice of conviction. I then announced that

"_____" would be converting to the bride's religion and had consented to proceed with the tradition of her church and would now be circumcised under the Law.

He reluctantly turned his back to the congregation at which time the muffled laughter could faintly be heard. Even I had not seen the "ceremonial tools" that the best man had placed under the cleanly pressed linen cloth. The bride and best man began chanting something which had clearly been rehearsed and at the same time began to slowly move their hands to remove the cloth.

The groom must have had his eyes closed because when he finally realized what he was seeing—I thought he was going to faint. There on the table, laid a pair of large butcher's poultry shears, a pair of construction gloves along with a box of band aids. His eyes attempted to make contact with mine, so I closed mine as if in prayer. I was told his bride kept a loving stare from start to finish and that his best man kept giving him pats of encouragement on the shoulder.

What seemed to last forever for me was when the best man couldn't contain his laughter any longer. His bride leaned over, gently kissed him on the cheek and said "And to think this is just day one!"

I've assisted in many practical jokes over the years, but I do believe this one was one of the best!

Just Another Day in Paradise

I don't believe there is another day, other than the birth of a child, that a man and woman could not be happier or more nervous, than on their wedding day. Such was the case of a couple I'm going to refer to as Jack and Jill.

They were both very young, about nineteen and twenty, if I remember correctly. The groom barely shaved. His moustache could have been trimmed with fingernail clippers, and he was visibly shaken from the first time he reached to shake my hand. His palms were sweaty and he gripped my hand as though he was holding on for dear life. I could see clearly the he was going to be the first groom I've ever had to either throw up or pass out. It was almost at a comedic level, but I felt so badly for this young kid that all I could do was console him and let him know that everything was going to be just fine.

I answered all his questions.

"What if I mess up?"

"You can't mess up—it's your wedding. How can you mess it up?"

"What if I forget what to say?"

"All you have to do is repeat after me. We'll go slowly."

"What if I drop the ring?"

"Pick it up."

After fifteen minutes of excuses I came right out and asked him if he was trying to get out of getting married.

"No—not at all."

I let him know he had a beautiful bride waiting for him to take her hand in marriage in about ten more minutes. Was he ready for it?

With grit in his teeth, his jaw clenched like Rambo, he looked me in the eyes and said, "Yes—yes I'm ready!"

We stepped out to the area where it was just the two of us. He walked out of the building like a Green Beret. The longer we stood and waited the more his confidence waned. I received the phone call from the coordinator letting me know that when the music changed, we could go. Silence prevailed for just a brief moment. Fear came over the groom. I laid my hand on his shoulder and said "Are you ready?"

The proverbial "deer in the headlight" look came over him, and once again, I reassured him that his bride was waiting on him. He took a deep breath, I shook his hand, and we began our approach to the place where he would take his wife's hand in marriage.

I smiled at his family as we walked up the aisle. Amazingly, they shared the same fearful look on their faces as the groom. I must have had a puzzled look on my face as we stood there waiting on his bride. Was I supposed to know something the rest of the guests already knew?

The wedding party marched out—three well-dressed men escorting three beautiful young ladies followed by a young lady tossing rose petals marking the path for the bride.

The all-familiar "Canon in D" began to play and as the image of the bride came into view. The groom leaned forward, took one glance, and turned his back to the crowd.

He proceeded to hurl his breakfast and dinner from the night before in an array that would have brought the Olympic judges holding cards that read "10" just for distance alone!

One woman jumped up from her seat and ran toward the bride and her father in an attempt to slow her approach. The bride stopped, listened attentively, and then sped up her pace.

I handed the groom a tissue which I normally reserve for tears. He wiped his mouth, dried his eyes on his jacket sleeve and with a look of embarrassment, turned and faced his bride. Before I was able to say anything, she spoke aloud "It's alright honey, I puked too!"

I reached into my pocket, handed them both a breath mint and began the ceremony. All I could do was hope that the groundskeeper hosed down the area behind me before the next wedding.

Just another day in paradise!

A Changed Woman

*I*t had to have been one of the hottest recorded days in Las Vegas history. I know it was mine— 122°, and performing an outdoor wedding does have its challenges in these conditions. People who are not used to the desert climate sunburn very easily and dehydrate in an hour. It can be dangerous to anyone who has any kind of medical condition.

I do my best to let my brides know that once their audience is seated; they need to proceed out as quickly as possible. Such was the case with one bride who insisted on several readings for their ceremony. A normal ceremony will last around 12-15 minutes once the couple is standing before me. Any longer than that and I must have stuttered! With the additional readings this woman wanted—we were looking upwards of 20-30 minutes; especially since the two of them wrote their own vows.

I had seen the groom's notes—short and to the point. I had not yet seen the bride's vows which were being carried on a satin pillow in an envelope by the Maid of Honor. The ceremony began and I was diligent in reading the requested verses, chapters and poems.

Wearing black, I was probably more aware of the temperatures than most anyone else present. Two o'clock in the desert shows mercy on no one. The groom placed the wedding band on his bride's ring finger, and it was the first time I had noticed something different about this young lady. Her hands were dripping perspiration at an alarming rate from her arms down to her fingertips.

I glanced up to see a woman who was so hot that her makeup was streaking down her face. Layer upon layer of tan and orange pools slowly made their way from her cheekbones down to her neckline—much like the movement of a glacier falling into an icy sea. The groom recited his vows with much haste, gently leaned closer to her and whispered "Your face is falling off."

In what I thought would be an absolute mental melt down, she merely smiled, took his handkerchief from his extended hand and said, "I want to marry you. I take you to be my husband."

The Maid of Honor handed her the rather bulging envelope and instead of reading it, she merely handed it to her new husband. She turned to me and simply said, "Let's wrap this up—I've got to wash my face."

I pronounced them husband and wife. I offered her some of the tissues I keep in my book which she gladly accepted. She wiped the makeup and sweat from her face, she turned and kissed her husband, and as they made their way down the aisle it was apparent, she was a *changed woman!*

It Ain't Always Easy

*T*here have been times when the wedding couple doesn't make it easy on me. I recall performing a wedding for a co-worker's stepson. He was a bit of a wild child and it was apparent that between him and his friends, he hadn't had much in his life.

Someone gave the couple, as a wedding present, a corner suite at a very well-known casino tower to have their ceremony. It didn't take long to find out that the groom wasn't picking up the tab for the affair since every kid in the room was emptying the well-stocked refrigerator. As I entered the room, my eyes were almost beginning to shed tears with the all-so-familiar scent of onions permeating the kitchen! I looked over to see the hors d'oeuvres on a plate, and I really couldn't believe what I was seeing. There, stacked neatly on a plate, were at least six hamburgers—quartered and with a toothpick in each piece. All the french fries were on a plate to themselves mounded up, which resembled many pictures I've seen on popular crime scene television programs of the human brain! It was easy to see that these had been put out for a few hours since the grease in them had set up and it would be a chore to peel them apart.

"Don't judge!" I scolded myself. I stood back and found a small grin covering my face. In walked the groom.

"Do you have your license?" I asked. He opened his billfold and showed me his driver's license.

"No sir—your marriage license."

"Yeah—we bought it," was his response.

"I need to have it so I can sign it and get it recorded with the State," I responded.

"You mean I gotta have that today?"

"I have to have it before I perform the wedding; I told you on the phone that I can't do the ceremony without it."

"Hey dude, we live in North Las Vegas and we left it on the counter in the kitchen . . . if I give you the keys—will you go get it?"

My patience wearing thin and after taking a deep breath, I let him know I wasn't going to leave and they needed to have someone go get it and bring it back. The groom and his cousin left to go get the license. I stepped out on the balcony patio and there was a stench that was all-too-familiar coming from the suite above. Apparently someone had gotten sick up there and attempts to clean it up were "stirring the pot," so to speak. I looked out across the Las Vegas Valley looking forward to the evening since my wife and I were going to go to a concert that night.

And as I stared at the beautiful Red Rock Mountains to the west, I noticed the color of the sky beginning to change. It was getting close to sunset. I glanced at my watch and the wedding was to take place in 15 minutes. The bride was still getting ready—not all of the family had arrived and the groom was still not back from his license run!

I placed a call to my wife to let her know we probably won't catch the opening act. Later I would find out that was an understatement.

A half-hour later, in came my co-worker and her husband. I explained what had been going on and asked for their assistance in expediting the ceremony. The first thing I heard from her mouth was "What is that putrid smell?"

I pointed to the "burgers" and she just shook her head and took the platter and placed it outside the door in the hallway. I believe she thought the mountain of fries was a sculpture so it was left alone.

Twenty more minutes went by and the groom returned with the envelope. "Who put my burgers outside?" he asked as he brought them back in and placed them on the counter beside the brain sculpture.

I do not believe I have ever filled out a marriage license as quickly as I did that evening. I asked where we were going to perform the actual ceremony and the groom pointed outside to the balcony.

It was going to be a very brief ceremony, so I figured I could stand the smell for just a few minutes longer. Another fifteen minutes later and we were all in place. No lights at my end of the balcony, so my cell phone doubled as a flashlight so I could read the ceremony. Out walked the bride in her beautiful white gown—and a baby bump that let me know there was a good possibility she would deliver before the service was over!

As she approached, water began to rain down from the balcony above. The maids took a bucket of water to rinse down the remains from the party the night before.

The bride, in all her beauty and elegance turned her Cuban temper to those above, and although I have absolutely no idea what was said, her soon-to-be husband smiled and said "You tell 'em mama!"

Ten minutes later, the two shared their first kiss as husband and wife and I was more than ready to leave. I hated to have to do it, but I pulled the groom aside and had to ask for my fee. He asked me to wait just a minute "I gotta hit up my homies." I shrugged as he went from man to man. He folded the cash, shook my hand and palmed it to me.

I put it in my pocket and left. As I was taking the elevator down to the lobby, I took it out and realized that I just got stiffed of over half my fee! Part of me was telling me to go back and get the rest of it. The other part told me it was a lesson learned and to go enjoy the evening with my wife.

The Haircut

O kay, here's the deal. I'm busy—I stay busy. I've got a recording studio and a ministry. I built and maintain my own websites and I also enjoy taking care of my own yard as well. I perform weddings and I schedule all of it myself. I write custom vows for couples and I make sure that their special day is just that—the most special it will ever be. I seem to live and breathe on the computer. I arrive early at every wedding because I believe that's what should be done. I didn't become #2 by slouching—I give it my all.

My wife and I swap the dry cleaner duties so I've always got my marryin' clothes ready to go. The few things she can't do for me are showers, shaving, and haircuts. Now, I do have one of the most awesome hair stylists in all of Las Vegas who cuts my hair and as a matter of fact, I performed her and her husband's wedding. Jamie is a beautiful and talented lady who has a quick wit and whose salon is located close to one of the more popular wedding gardens where I perform ceremonies. All I've got to do is remember to call her and schedule an appointment a couple of hours before a ceremony and I'm good. Easier said than done!

I was rushed for time—I had purchased one of those do-it-yourself clippers that had the adjustable head for different lengths. I can do this! I clipped and clipped and combed, and when I was done I realized that I had given myself a very professional looking haircut. At my age, I don't have much of it left so when it begins to get a bit long, it starts to resemble the dreaded comb-over. A short spikey look works best and I just achieved it! Jamie would be proud!

So here I went—talking to the nervous groom. After five minutes, he was calm, confident and ready to walk proudly down the aisle to marry his childhood sweetheart. I met with the bride—also timid and a bit scared. A few words of encouragement; I mentioned how handsome her groom was and how excited he was to hold her hand and exchange vows, and her tears were replaced with a glow like no other. She hugged me, her mom thanked and hugged me, and her daddy shook my hand with a huge smile on his face.

The time had come! The groom walked beside me with his chest thrown out like a professional wrestler beaming with pride. We walked past the crowd and took our place as we awaited the rest of the wedding party. Five handsome and well groomed men walked five beautiful ladies two at a time. They were followed by a young man no more than five years old with a $40 haircut and wearing a tuxedo. Behind him walked a precious little ten-year-old flower girl. Her tan was enviable; her dress was white with the same color red on a ribbon in her hair that matched the bridesmaids' gowns. Her eyes were practically copper colored. She carefully dropped rose petals for the entrance of the bride.

Enter the bride and her father. This entire ensemble was picture perfect. The father was holding back a tear as I asked who gives this woman's hand in marriage. The bride's smile was stellar! The entire ceremony was one that you could revisit on video many times over. As the service came to an end—I shook the hands of the parents from both sides of the families and proceeded to the reception hall to say hello to the disc jockey who is a good friend of mine. We stood and talked for a few moments. I turned to accept a few adulations of appreciation for a ceremony well done. My attention turned back to my friend; he asked "Did you cut your own hair today?"

Shock and fear overcame my entire mind and I responded "Maybe . . . Why?"

He stated there was a strand about 3 inches long and about the width of a pencil that I had missed. You have to know that everywhere I had walked and everyone I had spoken with raced through my mind. I handed him my pocket knife and told him to cut it off as quickly and as discreetly as possible. (Note to self: always keep your knife sharpened!) He hacked and chopped but to no avail. The same crowd of people, who saw me walk up the aisle with the groom, was now passing me once again. I waited there with my back against the wall and slithered out the side door as unobtrusive as possible.

I now call Jamie and no longer cut my own hair!

Quotes from the Dads

- "Deflower her gently"
- "Take her . . . and hurry"
- "I'll need her back on holidays with the grandkids"
- "Keep her . . . she's your tax deduction now."
- "Never raise a hand to her—or I will to you."
- "My daughter . . . is your problem now"
- "She told me walking out here that she's going to have a baby. We'll talk later."
- "Her mom's gonna miss her more than me - HERE!"
- "I already told her it's okay if we go hunting on weekends."
- "I'm not wild about you—but I am about her."
- "Take care of her."
- "You'll always be my baby."

- "Stay with him honey—you know he's got money."

The Rings?

*I*t was a classic wedding—both the bride and groom had been previously married. Both knew what they wanted in one another and had found it. Both were beyond 40 and were excited about this very special day. A lot of the planning was done together, the music, the location; the venue was very appealing to them. However, for a wedding minister to have to compete over the crowd in the adjacent room of a famous German restaurant seemed a bit overwhelming at first. It almost became a challenge over the constant "bier toasts" that echoed through the building.

The groom played music through the small amplifier from his tablet and the wedding party soon entered the room. The music was silenced by the unplugging of the tablet followed by a very familiar scratchy and electronic thumping sound. It brought a smile to each face in the room. As the bride made her entrance, I could hear the groom repeatedly murmuring "Oh crap."

Over and over as his bride approached—the words continued. He leaned over and asked me if I could stall the ceremony. I let him know it was not a good time to get sick! He smiled and said, "I'm not gonna run—I left the rings in the truck!"

I looked at him and smiled, encouraging him by letting him know it would be alright. As soon as the two stood face to face with one another, he said "I left the rings in the truck." The bride smiled and said, "We can use this one and carefully took her engagement ring off her finger and handed it to him. However, he had none. By this time, the entire wedding party noticed what had happened and began to mouth the issue to friends in the audience.

Laughter erupted and we continued with the ceremony. "You may now kiss your bride!" I finally exclaimed and as I pronounced them husband and wife and announced them, they walked back down the aisle . . . and kept going . . . all the way out of the room. The music stopped and the query "Where did they go?" filled the room.

I simply said, "He probably went out to the truck to get the rings!" Indeed, that's where he went. I met them in the lobby of the restaurant where I had him put her band on her finger and she placed his on him. Another kiss and they were on their way for photos.

Hey guys . . . don't forget the rings!

Gone Fishin'

I've been asked on several occasions what is the strangest wedding ceremony I've ever performed. Not certain what they considered the definition of "strangest"—but certainly there were some more memorable than others. I believe the most bizarre I've been asked to perform was in a shark tank in a hotel/casino here in Las Vegas. The groom sent me an email through my website and requested the possibility of it.

Okay—here's my deal. I'm not a diver, but with the tank only being about 20 feet deep and with me in a diver's suit, I didn't have a problem wearing a helmet and performing the wedding. I was told there are divers that go into the tank several times a day and hand feed the sharks. A false level of comfort rose and I was really getting excited about performing this wedding. I quoted the couple a price and made sure the date was clear in my schedule. They informed me a representative of the hotel/casino would be in touch.

Within a few days, I received an email from the establishment. Unfortunately, I needed to be a certified diver to enter the tank (in addition to waivers signed in the presence of their attorney and notary public). I considered getting my certification just to be able to say publicly "I did it!"

I visited the location the very next day and as I watched the diver feed one of the sharks—it literally ripped the food out of the man's hand.

I felt good about the choices that were made. I enjoy fishing more now, than ever before.

Free Ride in the Rain

*L*as Vegas is a city that is surrounded by mountains. "The Valley" as it is known to many locals boasts magnificent sunrises and sunsets due to the sun rising and lowering behind these mountains. These same mountains oftentimes block a lot of the rain clouds into the area; thus limiting the annual rainfall to approximately 4 inches of precipitation per year. When it does rain in Las Vegas, it usually comes down hard and heavy for short periods of time. Flooding is a common occurrence and becomes quite deadly at times. Rumor has it that if it rains on your wedding day, it is said to be good luck. In the years I have been performing weddings in the Las Vegas Valley, I have only been caught during two of them.

The first was barely to be considered a rain shower— light sprinkling, and everyone laughed that it could possibly rain in the desert. The second occasion was quite different.

The wedding couple hailed from the state of Washington. They were accustomed to getting at least half of our annual rainfall in a decent downpour in a single afternoon. The clouds had gathered and the sun was hidden behind them. The wedding coordinator told the bride that if the ceremony didn't begin soon, "the bottom would pour out!"

The bride delayed even longer thinking she would outwait the weather. The guests had all arrived and were sitting in a gazebo—staring at the ominous threats overhead. The groom and I walked at a faster than normal pace to our assigned positions.

New music began as the wedding party stepped gingerly to their places and as the music changed to the wedding march, the bride exited the building. Her dress was magnificent; a collar that rode high up her neck and was adorned with beads, and lace. This was also the longest train on any wedding dress I'd seen to date. She was "Front Cover Perfect!"

The walk from the building to the altar was a distance of about 150 feet. At the foot of the gazebo walkway, a tremendous flash of light and the immediate sound of thunder indicated that lightning had struck close by. The bride, visibly shaken instructed everyone "STAY PUT! I'M GETTING MARRIED!"

Not a drop of rain came from the sky; until I pronounced them husband and wife. As the groom kissed his bride and I announced them by their new names, I don't believe the rain could have fallen any harder. The bride hollered "We're married—get out of here!"

As everyone scattered I reached behind me, took my umbrella and watched as the bride, groom, wedding party and guests all got soaked. As the bride kicked off her high heels to run, she attempted to gather up this long wet rag of a dress. The groom was wearing rented patent leather shoes and quickly realized you cannot run in wet grass with slick bottom shoes. Gravity caught up with his clumsiness and he was soon on the ground alongside his best man and others.

With the fear of a lightning strike, the bride made her way back towards the reception hall. She pulled her way into the building practically out of breath and cold. She couldn't believe the dress could possibly weigh as much as it did; until she turned around to notice her flower girl had tripped and landed on the lengthy train. Being all of about 5 years old, all she could do was giggle and enjoy the ride.

The Brawlers

I'm not really sure how to describe the events from this ceremony. When I arrived, there were several men in suits and tuxedos exchanging cash. I couldn't tell if someone was going to make a liquor store run or gather a last minute gift for the wedding couple. It didn't take long to figure it out. Amazingly, the bridesmaids were doing the same, but only saying the words out loud.

"I got ten bucks she does!"

"No way—not on her wedding day—I'll cover that one!"

Still wondering what was going on, I overheard one of the guys, and as he saw me closing in on the crowd, he quickly put the cash in his pocket. One of the guys said "BUSTED." They began to tell me that the bride had a pretty good temper; she always said what was on her mind and that today would be no different. Everyone was betting on whether or not she would speak her mind. I just gave a smile and let them know it was her wedding and she could pretty much do anything she liked. Then the question was posed "What about him?" It was then that I realized this was going to be a one-sided issue. I was hoping that it would be a comical event versus a call to 9-1-1.

The proud husband-to-be and his groomsmen were in place. The groom had a smile of approval from all in attendance. The bridesmaids and the flower girl had just arrived and everyone was in perfect formation.

The traditional wedding march was chosen, and within moments, the proud father walked his daughter down the aisle. She was definitely a stunning bride.

I remember how well she fit in her dress and that the train stretched several rows of seats behind her as she made her entrance. Her face was soft and almost angelic. Her beaming father kissed her cheek to bid her farewell to her groom. As her future husband took her hand and led her to the spot the vows would be recited, she handed her wedding bouquet to her maid of honor and whispered "Did Daddy mess up my makeup with his kiss?"

The bridesmaid quickly shook her head "no," and she turned to face her man. As the ceremony began, she reached across and straightened his tie and adjusted his corsage. Everyone laughed a little under their breath, but it was apparent that absolutely no one had any intention of setting this woman off.

They had informed me that they did not want to write their own vows, but to simply use the "Traditional Ones" most commonly used. In this scenario, the couple repeats a few lines at a time after me. He went first—put the platinum band on her hand alongside an extremely healthy looking engagement ring, and said his vows to her. She looked at him softly and intently as we began the same for him.

She slid the band on his ring finger, repeated the same vows as he had said and then proceeded to continue on her own. The intensity of her smile waned and I could see her brow begin to wrinkle just a bit.

I can't recall the exact words she used, but certain things like "there will be no dogs in the house" and "you know I don't like sports" began to fill the air.

I was praying that the expression on my face hadn't changed from somber to shock as she continued with her soliloquy which ranged from new house shopping to his wardrobe. It's amazing how just a few short minutes can seem like an hour!

When she completed her speech, she looked at me and said "I'm through now, please continue." The angelic face and smile returned.

She looked longingly into his eyes and they shared a passionate kiss at the appropriate moment. As they began their recessional march from the altar, I noticed to my right a few of the bridesmaids giving one another 'high-fives.' To my left—cash was once again exchanging hands among the groomsmen. I shook my head, smiled, and remember saying to myself,

"If I ever write a book ... "

Epilogue

I f someone had told me 30 years ago I would become a minister and I would be preaching the Gospel of Jesus Christ, I would have probably responded negatively and with a few expletives to boot! I had my life where I thought I wanted it—I had learned a good trade in the plumbing and mechanical industry, always had a second job either as a woodworker (where the hobby becomes profitable) or as a club disc jockey or in a band.

Being center stage seemed comfortable to me. I had the ability to make people laugh and it worked for me. However, in my personal life, I was drowning in a sea that left misery in its path. No matter what I did, each and every time I took the helm of my own ship I ran it aground. It took me many years and tears to realize that. I had also realized that the path of misery I was leaving behind was also a trail for others to walk in as well. I preached my first message when I was 57 years old. By this time, I had once again surrendered my life to Jesus. What I had said some 30 years earlier was going to be my walk of life until the day I died.

I knew I would need help with it and asked God to send me an angel to help me with my walk. I was only asking figuratively. I had no intention of ever again being joined in marriage.

My wife holds many things dear to her heart; her kid's drawings and report cards through the years, her grandmother's Bible she still reads daily, our marriage license which hangs proudly on the wall, and the two page letter I sent her containing all the reasons I would never again marry. Living for Jesus is more fun than going to the casinos on Sunday. I never lose living for Jesus.

Being asked to pastor a ministry was one of the scariest times in my entire life. I've let myself down, I've let my wife and friends down and yes, I know I've let God down as well. Here is an opportunity to really mess up and say something wrong from the Bible.

I remember that I asked God to send me an angel and He did. My weaknesses are her strengths. My shortfalls are her strong points. He sent me an angel to compliment me, to raise me up and to love me. Little did I know that her prayers were being answered at the same time. God is good. We live for Him. Our home exemplifies Him. We sing honor and praise to Him. I have fun at my job. I love being "the one" who was asked to perform the marriage of couples beginning their lives together.

From the Couples

"Hello Jimmy!   Here are the pictures I promised you from our wedding on Friday Sept 17th. Thank you for making our special day even better! I will send more with you actually in them soon if you are interested! Everything was just PERFECT!!!!!"

—Steven and Allison

"Jimmy and Lori,   Thank you both so much for being a part of our wedding and thank you Jimmy for performing our ceremony and your amazing speech. You really blessed that day and our marriage and we can't thank you enough. You both are two beautiful people and have blessed my life. Thank you for everything. Love always and God bless!"

—Michelle and Cory

"Thank you for a beautiful ceremony we will remember it forever. I have attached some photos of the day. We all appreciated the way you put us at ease as some of us were very very nervous. The

surroundings were perfect for the photos afterwards. Thank you once again."

—Janet & Paul

"Pastor Jimmy performed our wedding for us. We were scared and wondered if we were doing the right thing. We had no idea he would counsel us but we asked him and he obliged. He's a good guy. He really cared about us and what our future together would be. We both used to go to church and we go again now. We can't tell you enough how much your words meant to us and how much more we are in love because of what you said about God. Thank you."

—James and Cheryl

"You will never ever know how much we appreciated you on the day we got married. Both of our mothers were driving us crazy! The fact that you told them both in such a loving way that today was OUR day and they should give hugs and confirmation and love. I've never seen my own mom look so astonished yet so accepting as I did at that moment. THANK YOU - THANK YOU! We love what you did for us!"

—Barry and Kaitlin

"Hey Jimmy – here we are married three years and already thinking about renewing our vows if for no other reason – just to come back to Vegas and see you again. It was fun the first time – just know it would be a magnificent party the second. Mum sends her best but doesn't think she would make the flight back across the pond again. Missing you in England and hope to travel again soon."

—James and Ashleigh

GOOD ADVICE

My advice for a successful marriage is a simple one.
Oftentimes I preach this to myself.
Keep God the center of your marriage.
Learn to forgive quickly.
Respect one another.
Every morning when you wake up ~
Fall in love all over again

About the Author

I am an ordained minister who has been performing weddings for four years in Las Vegas ~ The Wedding Capital of the World. I once had a country band that performed on the world-famous Las Vegas Strip under the name of the Brazos River Band; I have a concealed handgun permit and have been dubbed "The Pistol Packin' Preacher."

I allow my brides and grooms to let their hair down and have fun. I just never imagined how much fun they could have until all their private thoughts made their way out of their mouths!

I am married to a stunning and beautiful wife and have been pastor of a ministry at an assisted living senior center for the several years.

—Rev. James "Jimmy Mac" McNamara
www.jimmymacvegas.com